weight

Author
Jacqueline Dineen

Consultant
Freddi Freemantle
(ILEA Maths Co-ordinator)

Wayland

Starting Maths

Numbers
Shapes
Weight
Adding
Measuring
Taking Away

Series Editor: Deborah Elliott
Editor: Amanda Earl

First published in 1990 by
Wayland (Publishers) Limited
61 Western Road, Hove,
East Sussex, BN3 1JD, England

© Copyright 1990 Wayland (Publishers) Limited

British Library Cataloguing in Publication Data
Dineen, Jacqueline
    Weight.
    1. For children
    I. Title   II. Series
    531'.14

HARDBACK ISBN 1-85210-952-1

PAPERBACK ISBN 0-7502-0585-7

Typeset by Nicola Taylor, Wayland
Printed by Rotolito Lombarda S.p.A., Italy
Bound by Casterman S.A., Belgium

All the words that appear in **bold** are explained in the glossary on page 30.

Contents

Do you think elephants are heavy or light?

Elephants are very heavy.

They are the heaviest animals in the world.
How would you feel if an elephant stood on
your foot?

How would you feel if your friend stood on
your foot?
It would not hurt so much.
Your friend is not as heavy as an elephant.

Look around you for some heavy objects.
Are stones heavy? How do you know?
What other things did you find?

Could you lift these weights?

Some things are so heavy that you can't lift them at all.

This man is very strong. He can lift the weights.

You could not lift them off the ground.

Could you lift an elephant?
Could you lift a house?
Could you lift a car?

What other things are too heavy to lift?

What would happen if the balloon-seller let go of the balloons?

They would float away.

Some things are very light.
The balloons are filled with air.
They are so light that they fly away in the wind.
Kites fly in the wind too.

Can you think of other things which are very light?

Are **feathers** light?
Is paper light?
Will they fly away in the wind?

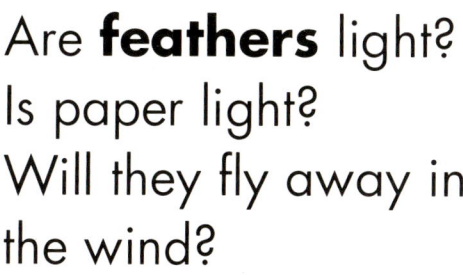

What do you think would happen if this boat was made of rock?

It would sink.

Some things are light enough to float on water.

Wood feels quite heavy when you pick it up.
It is heavier than a feather.
It is heavier than a balloon.

It would not float away in the air.
It is light enough to float on water.

Look at the picture. Find other things which float.

This bird is very big.
How can it fly?

The bird can fly because it is light for its size.

The bird is bigger than the stone.
Is the bird heavier than the stone?

The bird could not fly if it was as heavy as the stone.
One reason it can fly is that its feathers are light.

Large things can be lighter than smaller things.
Can you find things which are large and light?
Can you find things which are small and heavy?

Do you think this aeroplane is heavy?
We need to know how heavy things are.

This aeroplane is made of a light metal.

It has to carry a lot of people and **luggage**.
What would happen if a big plane like this was made of a heavy metal?
It would not be able to fly.

Can you make an aeroplane that is light enough to fly?
What will you use to make your plane?
Will you use paper? Will you use stone?

What happens when you throw a paper aeroplane?
Does the wind blow it along?

What would happen to a stone aeroplane?

Why do you think this luggage is being weighed?

We weigh things to find out how heavy they are.

We weigh them on scales.
Scales measure the weight of things.

The luggage is weighed to make sure it is not too heavy for the aeroplane.

Find two stones.

Hold one stone in each hand.
Which stone do you think is heavier?
See if your friend agrees with you.

Find some **balance scales** and check if you are right.

Why do you think Clare is weighing the oranges?

She is making some marmalade. She weighs the oranges so that she puts the right amount in the recipe.

How else could she decide how many to use?
She could guess, but she might be wrong.
Weighing is the best method.
These girls are weighing butter and flour.

Use balance scales,
like in either picture,
and find some marbles
to use as weights.
Put weights in one pan
and put flour or sand in
the other pan.
Can you balance the
scales? What does this
tell you?

Can you see the weight marked on the sugar packet?

We buy most of our food by weight.

You can look at food packets and see exactly how much there is inside.

Can you find some packets?
Which packets feel the heaviest?
Which feel the lightest?

Can you tell by the numbers on them?
Use your balance scales to check if you were right.

How much do you want?
Cheese comes in all shapes and sizes.
The salesperson puts the price on the
cheeses.

He marks the price and the weight.

Now the customers know how much they will get and how much it costs.

Put ten marbles on your balance scales.
Weigh out 'ten marbles worth' of sand, stones and paper.

Is one pile bigger than the others?

How much do you weigh?

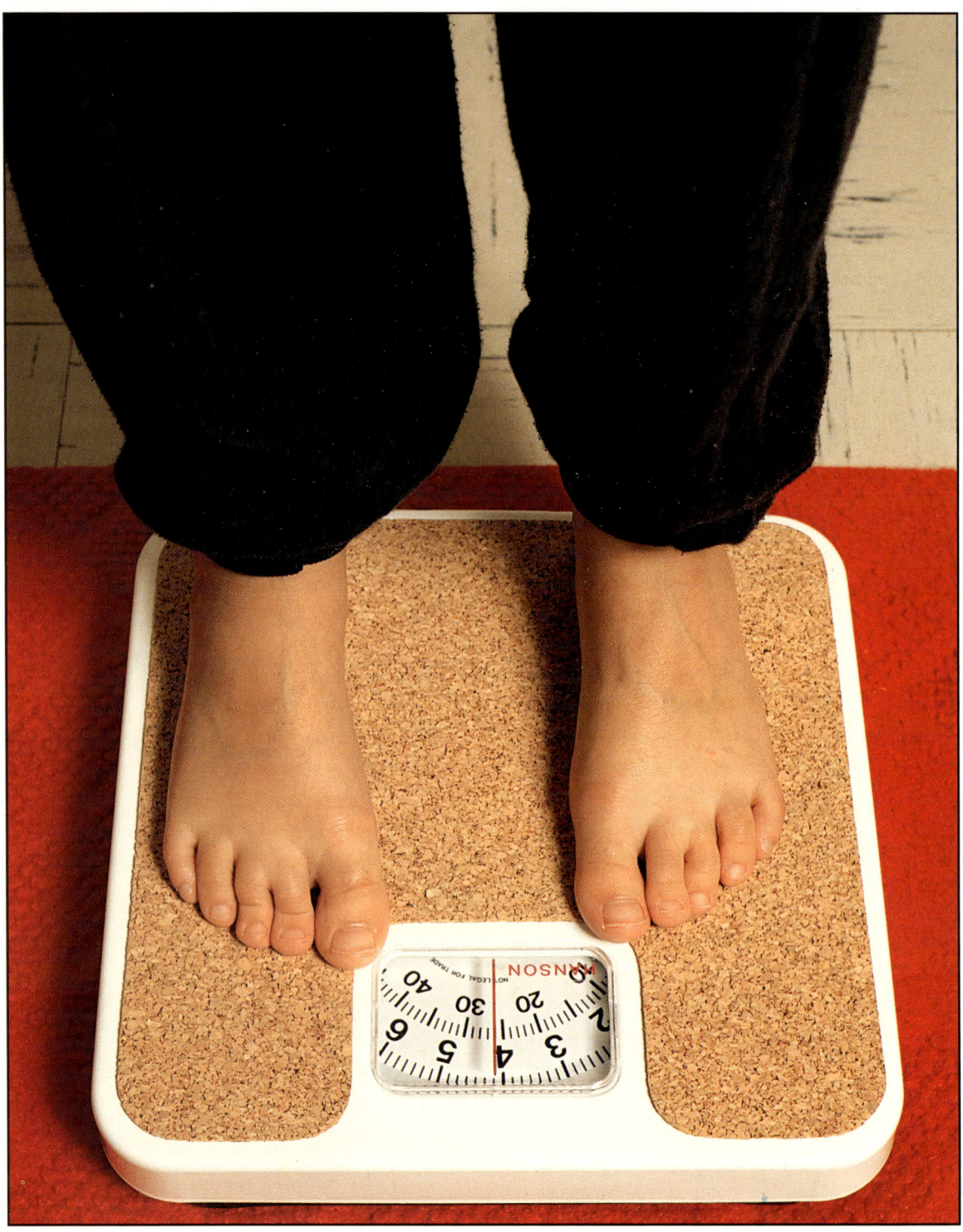

You can weigh yourself by standing on scales like these.

Why do people weigh themselves?
Healthy people should not be too heavy or too light.
The scales help them to check that they are the right weight.
Doctors weigh babies and small children to see if they are growing properly.

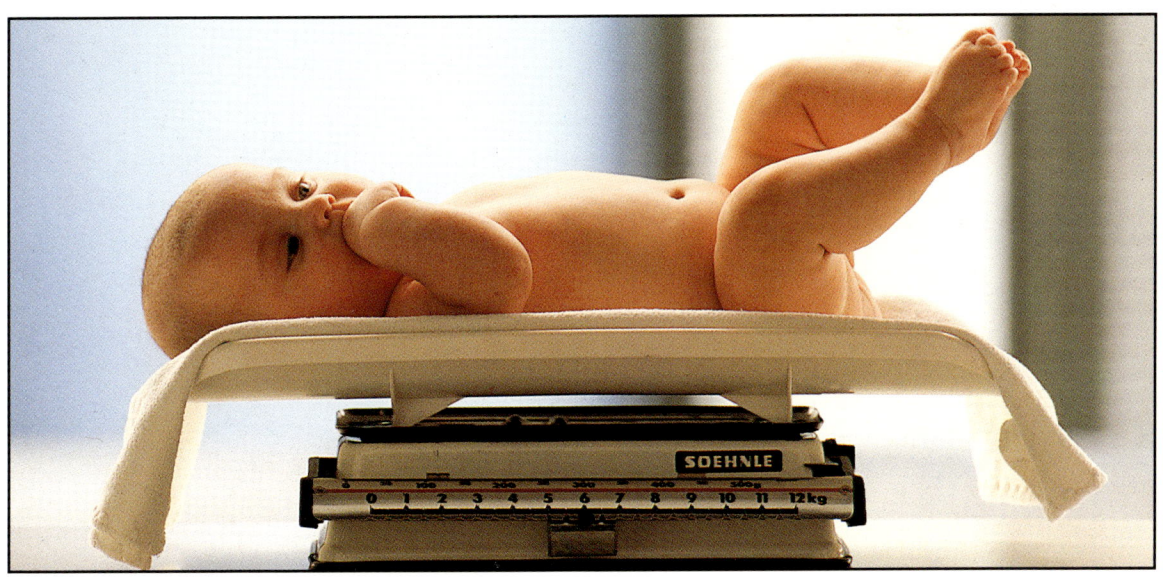

Weigh yourself. What do you weigh? What does your friend weigh?
Are you heavier than your friend?

Why do you think these parcels need to be weighed?

To find out how much it costs to send them.

It costs more to send a heavy parcel than it does to send a lighter parcel or a letter.
Some letters and parcels travel by aeroplane.

People often write **'air mail' letters** on special thin paper.
Why do you think they do this?

Big parcels are not always heavier than smaller parcels.
You can try this for yourself.

You need some parcels of different sizes.
Weigh them on your balance scales.

What would happen if this lorry was too heavy for the bridge?

The bridge would break.

We need to know how much weight the bridge can take.
We need to know how heavy the lorry is.
Weight is important in lots of ways.
We have seen some of them in this book.
Can you think of any more?
Find and then draw pictures of three heavy things and three light things.

Can you draw a picture to show what happens when something is too heavy?

Glossary

'Air mail' letters Letters which are sent by aeroplane and are usually written on very thin paper to make them as light as possible.

Balance scales An instrument for weighing, usually made of a swaying bar, with pans hanging at the ends. By balancing the pans, you know the objects being weighed are the same weight. Such scales are often used in schools.

Feathers The covering of a bird's body, needed for protection, like the fur on animals.

Luggage Suitcases and other bags, full of clothes and belongings, used when travelling.

Marmalade A slightly bitter jam made from fruits such as oranges and lemons.

Books to Read

Big and Little, John Satchwell (Walker Books, 1984).

Investigating Weight, Ed Catherall (Wayland, 1983).

Weighing and Measuring, Annabel Thomas and Nigel Langdon (Usborne, 1986).

Weight, Pluckrose and Fairclough (Franklin Watts, 1988).

Picture acknowledgements

The pictures in this book were supplied by the following: Bruce Coleman 4; Greg Evans 21, 28; Chris Fairclough 10, 16; Topham Picture Library12, 14; Tim Woodcock cover, 5, 7, 8, 9 (below), 11, 13, 15, 17, 18, 19, 20, 22, 23, 24, 26, 27, 29. All the illustrations are by Peter Bull Art.

Index